I Love You Just As You Are!

Written by Beth Rucker

Illustrated by Christine Sweet

All proceeds from this book are donated to Just Be You.
Learn more at justbeyou.org.

Illustrated by Christine Sweet | csweetfineart.com
Produced by Publish Pros | publishpros.com

To my children, I love you always.
To all the beautiful souls reading this book, I hope you
know you are loved just as you are!

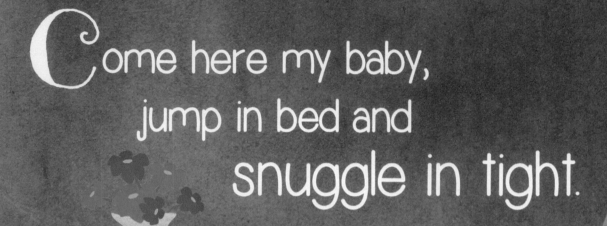

Come here my baby,
jump in bed and
snuggle in tight.

Before we say our prayers
and turn out the light...

Tell me my love what would you say
was the very best
part of your day?

Was it at the park and swinging on swings?

...playing with Mochi and pretending you have wings?

belly laughs and
hugs so tight...

or playing in the grass and soaking up the sunlight?

I love how you find
the simple magic in your days

and embrace who you are
and all your silly ways.

As you lie in bed and sleep under the stars, please know that

I love you just as you are!

I love you from the sky above
to the ground below.

This I hope you will always know!

Now close your eyes
and drift off to sleep,
here are some words
I want you to keep...

You are kind, funny and smart.

smart

caring

kind

silly

BIG heart

You will always be my
shining star and remember

I love you
just as you are!

Here are just some of the ways

I love you JUST AS YOU ARE!

An invitation to write what you love about your shining star.

About the Author

Beth Rucker spends her time with her family and dog, Mochi, in Charleston, SC and New York City. She is a mother, artist, and founder of Just Be You, a non profit dedicated to increasing kids' self-confidence and encouraging them to embrace their unique selves. This book was created in the hopes that as kids drift off to sleep, they are left with the words, "I love you just as you are." All proceeds from this book are donated to Just Be You.

About the Illustrator

Christine Sweet is a watercolor artist and illustrator based in Charleston, SC. She is best known for her winsome, modern renderings of coastal creatures but also deeply enjoys the diverse world of digital art. She co-owns Sweet Bros Games and serves as the Chief Art Director and Illustrator. Other than being creative, Christine's favorite thing to do is spend time with her husband, Brian, and three remarkable kids—Jersey, Zion, and Jackson.

CPSIA information can be obtained
at www.ICGtesting.com
Printed in the USA
JSHW071151170223
37865JS00003B/4